RIGHT STANDING, RIGHT LIVING

COMPREHENSIVE STEPS FOR ANYONE WHO WANTS
TO MAKE THE BEST DECISIONS FOR THEIR LIFE

EMMANUEL ATOE

WESTBOW
PRESS®
A DIVISION OF THOMAS NELSON
& ZONDERVAN

WestBow Press books may be ordered through booksellers or by contacting:

WestBow Press
A Division of Thomas Nelson & Zondervan
1663 Liberty Drive
Bloomington, IN 47403
www.westbowpress.com
844-714-3454

Scripture quotations are from the Holy Bible, King James Version (Authorized Version). First published in 1611. Quoted from the KJV Classic Reference Bible, Copyright © 1983 by The Zondervan Corporation.

Cover Design by Signs Madueke

ISBN: 978-1-6642-8767-9 (sc)
ISBN: 978-1-6642-8768-6 (e)

Print information available on the last page.

WestBow Press rev. date: 04/27/2023

SPONSORSHIP PAGE

THIS BOOK IS SPONSORED BY

....

....

AS A GIFT TO

....

....

ON THIS DAY

....

'Each one must give as he has decided in his heart,
not reluctantly or under compulsion,
for God loves a cheerful giver.'
(2 Corinthians 9:7, ESV)

DEDICATION

This book is dedicated to the Righteous in Christ

A special thanks go to those who love Right Living

The LORD bless you and keep you; The LORD make His face shine upon you and be gracious to you; The LORD lift His countenance upon you and give you peace, in Jesus' Name. Amen.

Always be full of joy in the Lord. I say it again - rejoice!

CONTENTS

INTRODUCTION

The eyes of the Lord are over His children.

> *"For the eyes of the Lord are over the righteous. and his ears are open unto their prayers."*
>
> — 1 PETER 3:12

RIGHTEOUSNESS IS THE FOUNDATION OF A HEALTHY RELATIONSHIP BETWEEN THE creator and the creature. A healthy relationship must be righteous for the ultimate satisfaction of the participants. God's love and grace have given to mankind through His divine power all things that pertain to life and godliness, through the knowledge of Him who called us by glory and virtue, by which we have been given exceedingly great and precious promises, that through these, we may be partakers of the divine nature, having escaped the corruption that is in the world through lust.

My friend the path of righteousness is life. The human mind cannot access the depth of God's infinite love for His creation. As the Psalmist says: What is man that You are mindful of him, And the son of man that You visit him? For You have made him a little lower than the angels, And You have crowned him with glory and honor. You have made him to have dominion over the works of Your hands; You have put all things under his feet. Mankind has been condemned due to rebellion but God, in His grace, offers us justification by faith in His Son, Jesus Christ.

When we are justified by God, we receive salvation, and we are redeemed from our sins, because of the blood of our Lord and Savior Jesus Christ. This is the good news for mankind, God's righteousness in His plan for salvation.

> *"For I am not ashamed of the gospel, for it is the power of God for salvation to everyone who believes, to the Jew first and also to the Greek. For in it the righteousness of God is revealed from faith to faith; as it is written, But the righteous man shall live by faith."*
>
> — ROMANS 1:16

Mankind is justified by faith to receive God's righteousness, which is demonstrated by transforming us from rebels to followers of Jesus. It does not matter how badly a person has messed things up in the past, or how many mistakes you have made. A born-again child of God should lift his [her head] higher knowing fully well that you are righteous, certainly not because of anything you've done but because of what you've received, by faith in Jesus, the very righteousness of God. That is awesome, my friend, because that is what God's word says about you. Take it, accept it, walk in the light of it and live it, because that is what you are in Christ Jesus.

Righteousness gives us the creative ability to be like the Creator in all ways throughout our lives.

> *"He who follows righteousness and mercy. Finds life, righteousness, and honour."*
>
> — PROVERB 21:21

This demands honesty, trust, and faithfulness. The almighty God is faithful, forever perfect, and omnipotent. The righteousness of God is God's everlasting faithfulness to His people; to fulfill His promises.

The Holy Scripture says in Hebrews 13:8 "Jesus Christ *is* the same yesterday, today, and forever." God's redemption is spiritual, but it deals with the complete aspect of the life of every human being who accept this great gift. There is power in the precious blood of our Lord and Saviour Jesus Christ. How much more shall the blood of Christ, who through the eternal Spirit offered Himself without spot to God, cleanse your conscience from dead works to serve the living God? And for this reason He is the Mediator of the new covenant, by means of death, for the redemption of the transgressions under the first covenant, that those who are called may receive the promise of the eternal inheritance.

God is concerned about the complete wholeness of mankind. God's original design and condition for humanity in creation is restored. There is absolutely nothing that can hinder the plan and purpose of the Almighty Father of Light, all-powerful, all-knowing God. The Holy Scripture confirms that heaven and earth may pass away but the Word of God stands for ever. Furthermore, God honors His word more than His name. Mankind falls and becomes slaves to sin but could not prevent God's plan of love, that was put in place by redemption through Christ because of His faithfulness.

2 Corinthians 5:21, "For He made Him who knew no sin to be sin for us, that we might become the righteousness of God in Him." The focus is primarily on attaining that moral perfection through Christ and maintaining it.

"For I am not ashamed of the gospel, for it is the power of God for salvation to everyone who believes, to the Jew first and also to the Greek."

— ROMANS 1:16-17

For in it the righteousness of God revealed from faith to faith; as it is written, "the righteous man shall live by faith." So, righteousness is also understood as God's faithfulness to fulfill His plan and purpose for mankind, and His creation, because as creator He loves His relationship with us.

ONE

RENEWED IN THE SPIRIT
OF YOUR MIND

> *"For I am not ashamed of the gospel of Christ, for it is the power of God to salvation for everyone who believes, for the Jew first and also for the Greek. For in it the righteousness of God is revealed from faith to faith; as it is written, The just shall live by faith."*
>
> — ROMANS 1:16-17

THE JUST LIVE BY FAITH. ALL HUMANS IS BORN INTO COMPLETE BONDAGE TO SIN. THE Adamic nature fulfilling the desires of the flesh and of the mind, and were by nature children of wrath, makes man unable to produce any sort of righteousness on our own. In truth, any attempt by any person to produce his [or her] own righteousness is absolutely disgusting or filthy in the eyes of God. Self-righteousness is morally or spiritually impure, like a polluted garment we have all become like unclean people, and all our righteous deeds are equally filthy in the presence of a Holy God. That's the reason we need a righteous Christ who has never committed any sin to take on Himself our sin, as a Divine substitute, so that in him we might become the righteousness of God. Righteousness is received by faith in the perfect holiness of Christ. The Character of God; makes Him always "The Right One". Therefore, sin is against God's plan and design for mankind, the only acceptable living standard of the heavenly Justice is God's righteousness which gives us the access to stand and be acceptable before the Holy God.

> *"For the wrath of God is revealed from heaven against all ungodliness and unrighteousness of men, who suppress the truth in unrighteousness, because what may be known of God is manifest in them, for God has shown it to them."*
> — ROMANS 1:18-19

We must be renewed in the spirit of our mind to pursue God's righteousness and not our self-righteousness. The scriptures says that we should.

> *"Flee also youthful lusts; but pursue righteousness, faith, love, peace with those who call on the Lord out of a pure heart."*
> — 2 TIMOTHY 2:22

Therefore, righteousness is something we should desire, because no individual is able to make it, we depend on our Lord Jesus to create it for us. Once you dare to accept that truth, your life will be forever changed, because you will no longer be satisfied until you take your rightful place beside Him, and learn to operate like Him. Receive the baptism of fire to stir up yourself, stand-up and step up to the position of authority that is yours in Christ Jesus.

By faith walking daily in the righteousness of God that was imputed on those who believe, through the atoning work that Jesus Christ accomplished on the cross. Jesus Christ lived a life of total obedient, to God because He was perfect in all ways, faultless and sinless life. The redemption of mankind could only be possible by the perfection of Christ who atoned for the sins of His people. The blood of Jesus Christ, the righteous is the only perfect sacrifice that could enter Heaven.

> *"Jesus said, Do not hold on to me, for I have not yet ascended to the Father. Go instead to my brothers and tell them, 'I am ascending to my Father and your Father, to my God and your God."*
>
> — JOHN 20:17

Thanks be to God that Jesus Christ had no sin, so we don't have to strive, struggle, and attain our own righteousness, because Himself bore our sins in His body on the tree, that we might die to sin and live to righteousness. The Church has come into righteous standing with God through reconciliation by Jesus. Therefore, awake to righteousness, and do not sin; for some do not have the knowledge of God.

> *"I will greatly rejoice in the Lord, My soul shall be joyful in my God; For He has clothed me with the garments of salvation, He has covered me with the robe of righteousness."*
>
> — ISAIAH 61:10

TWO

PUT ON THE NEW MAN

> *"Take delight in the Lord, and He will give us the desires of our heart."*
>
> — PSALM 37:4

As CHRISTIANS IT IS VERY ESSENTIAL WHAT WE BELIEVE AND HOW WE LIVE OUT those beliefs in our journey of Faith. The Word of God Word restores our soul. The Lord leads us in the paths of righteousness for His name's sake. (Psalm 23:3) Right living is based on Christ righteousness, to experience the presence of the Holy Spirit in practical ways throughout our Christian life. Sin made mankind to lack God's righteousness, but thanks be to our Lord Jesus, we receive God's righteousness when God justifies us by faith. At new birth we are made the righteousness of God in Christ and we are complete in Him, who is the head of all principality and power. (Colossians 2:10) We should take delight in the LORD, and he will give us the desires of our heart. The scripture says in Romans 3:23, "For all have sinned and fall short of the glory of God". God's plan of salvation is that those who put their faith in Jesus, receive the gift of righteousness. This is a gift from the heart of God's love because all have sinned and have becomes enemies of God and only deserve His wrath. There is no mankind that is holy and righteous able to save anyone or himself "There is none righteous, no not one" Romans 3:10.

The only Saviour is the Righteous Son of the living God, Jesus Christ. As the scriptures says for scarcely for a righteous man will one die; yet perhaps for a good man someone would even dare to die. But God demonstrates His own love toward us, in that while we were still sinners, Christ died for us. Much more then, having now been justified by His blood, we shall be saved from wrath through Him. Romans 5:7-9.

Mankind due to sin nature conducted us in the lusts of our flesh, fulfilling the desires of the flesh and of the mind, and were by nature children of wrath, could not stand before a Holy and Just God, could not justify himself, unable to obey the law and live in righteousness. And you He made alive, who were dead in trespasses and sins, so Christ came and lived in perfection in our place. For He (God) made Him (Christ) who knew no sin to be sin for us (Mankind), that we (Mankind) might become the righteousness of God in Him (Christ). 2 Corinthians 5:21. We are instantly and completely justified through that righteousness and made a "joint heir with Christ."

We are clothed in the robe of His righteousness because God so love mankind that He gave us Jesus as a substitute who took on Himself our sin or disobedience, nailed it to the cross, so that we can have His righteousness. What an awesome, amazing and perfect love of God. There is absolutely nothing that has the power to separate us from it.

Glory be to God that we can say with holy boldness like Apostle Paul, For I am persuaded that neither death nor life, nor angels nor principalities nor powers, nor things present nor things to come, nor height nor depth, nor any other created thing, shall be able to separate us from the love of God which is in Christ Jesus our Lord. Romans 8:38-39.

> *"I will greatly rejoice in the Lord, My soul shall be joyful in my God; For He has clothed me with the garments of salvation, He has covered me with the robe of righteousness, As a bridegroom decks himself with ornaments, And as a bride adorns herself with her jewels. For as the earth brings forth its bud, As the garden causes the things that are sown in it to spring forth, So the Lord God will cause righteousness and praise to spring forth before all the nations. The Gentiles shall see your righteousness, And all kings your glory. You shall be called by a new name, Which the mouth of the Lord will name. You shall also be a crown of glory. In the hand of the Lord, And a royal diadem In the hand of your God."*
>
> — ISAIAH 62:2-3

Desire righteousness and righteous living. Acknowledging daily who you're as a born-again child of God who has been made the righteousness of God, and desire to enjoy the benefits of the righteous. This will take you from a mindset of defeat to walk in the light of right standing with God. I will greatly rejoice in the Lord, my soul shall be joyful in my God; for He has clothed me with the garments of salvation, He has covered me with the robe of righteousness.

Without Jesus mankind is subject to the eternal consequences of sin. God's grace and love has given us a way out for salvation through the sacrifice of Jesus Christ. He gave His perfect life to make a way for us to be saved. Salvation satisfies the demands of God's law and His wrath against sin while at the same time showing God's grace and everlasting love for mankind. The purpose and plan of God was perfectly accomplished on the cross.

Therefore, the desire of our heart should be right living by turning away from our sinful paths and turning to our Savior. We should desire and choose His holy, righteous, and perfect way of life. The path is to always trust and obey Him who has provided for us eternal life. We should anchor our faith on Jesus Christ finished work and righteousness.

THREE

GOD'S DIVINE PLAN FOR US

"For I am not ashamed of the gospel of Christ, for it is the power of God to salvation for everyone who believes, for the Jew first and also for the Greek. For in it the righteousness of God is revealed from faith to faith; as it is written, The just shall live by faith."

— ROMANS 1:16-17

IT IS GOD'S DIVINE PLAN FOR HIS CHILDREN TO WALK IN RIGHTEOUSNESS. EVERY BORN-again believer must have a clear knowledge and understanding about what the righteousness of God is and how it is received. The word "righteousness" must be profound in the hearts of every believer. There must be no doubt or confusion regarding its meaning and how to receives it. Righteousness is very important because it affects our walk of faith. That is our right standing with God, because it is the condition of being in right relationship with the Lord. There are some believers who still don't have the knowledge of how they become right in the sight of God. The greatest deception of the power of darkness is to make the born the born-again believe that is it is through their actions that they can become righteous. Some Christians are wrongly convinced believing they can become righteous as they do good works, get older, rendering services, attend church services, stop some bad habits, assist others, pray hard, etc.

> *"And if by grace, then it is no longer of works; otherwise, grace is no longer grace. But if it is of works, it is no longer grace; otherwise, work is no longer work."*
> — ROMANS 1:6

My friends, God's divine plan has given us His righteousness by grace. This can only happen through the gift of faith and complete dependence upon the finished works of our Lord Jesus Christ. Jesus is the way and there is no other way. There is absolutely nothing of our action, anything we can do, work or action to obtain righteousness of God in Christ Jesus, We are born-again to be in right relationship with the Lord. Any form of self-righteousness action is deception and denial of the truth because there is a correlation between our actions and our right standing with God.

There is absolutely nothing that we can do to be made the righteousness of God or to be more righteous. Every born again must believe steadfastly in their hearts that whosoever accepts what Jesus has done for them by faith receives from our Lord the gift of righteousness. God's divine plan has given mankind the gospel of Christ, for it is the power of God to salvation for everyone who believes for in it the righteousness of God is revealed from faith to faith.

Therefore, the just shall live by faith. Faith in the Word of God is what leads us through the power of the Holy Spirit to a changed heart. Our mind renewed with the Spirit inspired Word of God brings about restoration of our soul that in turn changes our actions. Our heart is not changed by our dos and don'ts i.e., our actions because God's grace has given us a new heart according to the scriptures.

> *"I will give you a new heart and put a new spirit within you; I will take the heart of stone out of your flesh and give you a heart of flesh. I will put My Spirit within you and cause you to walk in My statutes, and you will keep My judgments and do them."*
>
> — EZEKIEL 36:26-27

FOUR

CROWN OF RIGHTEOUSNESS

> *"Henceforth there is laid up for me a crown of righteousness, which the Lord, the righteous judge, shall give me at that day: and not to me only, but unto all them also that love his appearing."*
>
> — 2 TIMOTHY 4:8

As Christians it is very essential what we believe and how we live out those beliefs. I am convinced that our focus in life should be looking unto Jesus Christ the author and finisher of our faith and trusting to receive the crown of righteousness i.e., the Victorious Church Crown that the Lord would place upon every member of the body, His victorious church because anyone who endures to the end shall be saved. God in his infinite grace have saved you through faith, and that not of yourselves; *it is* the gift of God, not of works, lest anyone should boast. For we are His workmanship, created in

Christ Jesus for good works, which God prepared beforehand that we should walk in them.

The desire of every believer should be to receive reward from our master and Lord Jesus Christ the victor's crown. That is why we are invited to run the race of faith. We must courageously by faith be determined to endure to the end, pursuing the plan and purpose of God for our lives. We must fight with boldness the "fight of faith" strengthened with might through His Spirit in the inner man. We shall succeed by the power that duels in us.

> *"Therefore we also, since we are surrounded by so great a cloud of witnesses, let us lay aside every weight, and the sin which so easily ensnares us, and let us run with endurance the race that is set before us, looking unto Jesus, the author and finisher of our faith, who for the joy that was set before Him endured the cross, despising the shame, and has sat down at the right hand of the throne of God."*
>
> — HEBREWS 12:1-2

The New Testament reveals that heavenly crown, will be awarded to believers. These are imperishable crown which are symbols of honor, dignity, and royalty. Every true follower of Jesus Christ should with joy in the heart look forward to the reward of receiving this victor's crown on the head from the Lord. However, we cannot have this reward by our own self-righteousness because no human being can attain any right standing with God through personal works, no matter how perfectly done, because our righteousness is as a filthy rag compared to God's righteousness. Good work is fine, and we are encouraged to do good, but we must not trust in our own goodness for right standing with God. Righteousness is a gift we receive from God through faith to enable us live a victorious Christian life

Therefore, our trust and total dependance should be on God through the finished work of our Lord Jesus.

> *"For thou preventest him with the blessings of goodness: thou settest a crown of pure gold on his head"*
> — PSALM 21:3

There are at least five Crowns mentioned in the scriptures. These are the Crown of Glory, Crown of Righteousness, Crown of Rejoicing, the Crown of Life, and the Crown of Gold. These promises are made by the Lord to victorious believers who endured to the end and finished their race of faith.

CROWN OF GLORY

> *"Shepherd the flock of God, which is among you, serving as overseers, not by compulsion but willingly, not for dishonest gain but eagerly; nor as being lords over those entrusted to you, but being examples to the flock; and when the Chief Shepherd appears, you will receive the crown of glory that does not fade away".*
> — 1 PETER 5:2-4

Another word for shepherd is Pastor. The pastor of a church, The congregation, or a minister of the gospel of Christ: A person who has received and obeyed, what the Lord has commanded us. And He said to them, Go into all the world and preach the gospel to every creature.

> *"Therefore, take heed to yourselves and to all the flock, among which the Holy Spirit has made you overseers, to shepherd the church of God which He purchased with His own blood. For I know this, that after my departure savage wolves will come in among you, not sparing the flock."*
>
> — ACTS 20:28

A pastor is a person who is anointed to feed the body of Christ, instructing them in spiritual things. The voice of God for the people in sermons. A diligent person who knows the state of the flocks and attend to their needs. God-given responsibility to care for the sheep.

In 2 Corinthians chapter 11, apostle Paul revealed his concern for believers faithfulness and some of his challenges and suffering for Christ: in prisons more frequently, in deaths often, from the Jews five times he received forty stripes minus one. Three times he was beaten with rods; once he was stoned; three times he was shipwrecked; a night and a day he has been in the deep; in journeys often, in perils of waters, in perils of robbers, in perils of his own countrymen, in perils of the Gentiles, in perils in the city, in perils in the wilderness, in perils in the sea, in perils among false brethren; in weariness and toil, in sleeplessness often, in hunger and thirst, in fasting often, in cold and nakedness.

> *"besides the other things, what comes upon me daily: my deep concern for all the churches."*
>
> — 2 CORINTHIANS 11:28

The Pastor is the leader of the local church government, provide leadership and most especially as a faithful shepherd provide dearly for the welfare and care for the flock of Jesus Christ. This Crown of Glory or the shepherd's Crown is the reward that will be given to faithful and obedient

Pastors who faithfully shepherd the church of God which He purchased with His own blood.

CROWN OF RIGHTEOUSNESS

"Finally, there is laid up for me the crown of righteousness, which the Lord, the righteous Judge, will give to me on that Day, and not to me only but also to all who have loved His appearing."

— 2 TIMOTHY 4:8

Although it is not explicitly stated in the scriptures, I am truly convinced that this crown is for those who with faith and holy living are expecting (as promised in the scriptures), the coming of our Lord and Saviour Jesus Christ. This is for those looking forward to the blessed hope and glorious appearing of our great God and Savior Jesus Christ, who gave Himself for us, that He might redeem us from every lawless deed and purify for Himself *His* own special people, zealous for good works.

The reward is with our Lord Jesus, to give to everyone according to his work and like little children, we must abide in Him, that when He appears, we may have confidence and not be ashamed before Him at His coming. In his letter to the church 2 Timothy 4:7-8 apostle Paul wrote about his hopeful expectation after death, A crown to be given to him by our Lord Jesus. He said that he had fought the good fight, he had finished the race, he had kept the faith.

Finally, He wrote there is laid up for me the crown of righteousness, which the Lord, the righteous Judge, will give to him on that Day, and not to him only but also to all who have loved His appearing.

Thank God, apostle Paul said that the Lord Jesus will give not to him only but also to all who have loved His appearing. So, this crown is prepared for everyone who lived holy lives in expectation and longing for the return of Jesus. However, there are specific indications of what apostle Paul declared that he had done, and if we can learn from him according to 1 Corinthians 11:1, "Be imitators of me, as I am of Christ". What must be done for anyone to receive the crown of righteousness as imitators of apostle Paul, as he is of Christ. There is a good fight to fight to receive the crown. Believers must fight the good fight.

> "Fight the good fight of the faith. Take hold of the eternal life to which you were called and about which you made the good confession in the presence of many witnesses."
>
> — 1 TIMOTHY 6:12

As believers we are called to run and finish the race to receive the crown of righteousness. God has given us the Holy Spirit to assist us walk, live, fulfill successfully on earth His plan and purpose for us.

> "Therefore, we also, since we are surrounded by so great a cloud of witnesses, let us lay aside every weight, and the sin which so easily ensnares us, and let us run with endurance the race that is set before us."
>
> — HEBREWS 12:1

In the case of apostle Paul, it was his calling and his ministry, the source of desire to finish with joy. As the body of Crist believers are also called to run the race and finish with joy. The goal should be to run the race empowered by the Holy Spirit and to finish the course successfully. This is what apostle Paul said regarding his race and desire to finish with joy.

> *"But none of these things move me; nor do I count my life dear to myself, so that I may finish my race with joy, and the ministry which I received from the Lord Jesus, to testify to the gospel of the grace of God."*
>
> — ACTS 20:24

We need faith to run the race. We are encouraged to keep the faith because human effort is limited, and lack of faith could lead to discouragement and failure. We must also endeavor to maintain the faith, because without faith it is impossible to please Him, for anyone who comes to God must believe that He is, and that He is a rewarder of those who diligently seek Him. Hebrews 11:6. We must strive to finish the course with success, without drawing back, fighting the good fight. As it is written the just shall live by faith; But if anyone draws back, My soul has no pleasure in him. But we are not of those who draw back to perdition, but of those who believe to the saving of the soul, Hebrews 10:38-39. We must hold fast without wavering our profession of faith.

CROWN OF REJOICING

> *"There is none righteous, no, not one; There is none who understands; There is none who seeks after God. They have all turned aside; They have together become unprofitable; There is none who does good, no, not one."*
>
> — ROMANS 3:10-12

Everyone that is not born again have failed to meet the requirements of the righteous law of God, the scripture calls such people as sinners. And unless they repent and receive Christ as Lord and Savior, they have chosen the state of "people without God" which is eternal separation from God. However, Jesus revealed to us in the scriptures.

> *"I say to you that likewise there will be more joy in heaven over one sinner who repents than over ninety-nine just persons who need no repentance."*
>
> — LUKE 15:7

There is joy in heaven over one sinner who repents, and the scripture speaks also of crown given to those who brought others to Jesus, that is the soul-winner's crown. Believers are commanded to go all over the world and witness, by sharing the good news of the Word of God with unbelievers. Salvation is only by grace through faith therefore the more people believers can reach with the good news of the gospel the better. Go into the world and preach the gospel to every creature before the return of our Lord Jesus.

> *"For God so loved the world that He gave His only begotten Son, that whoever believes in Him should not perish but have everlasting life."*
>
> — JOHN 3:16

Therefore, there is hope for the world, because there is joy in Heaven for everyone that repents from their sins and receives Jesus Christ as their Savior. Eternal life is the gift of God to anyone who simply believes in Jesus. So, anyone who shares and witness to unbelievers about God's love and help to win soul to the kingdom of God makes that person a candidate of the Crown of Rejoicing. So soul winning should be believers' most important goal. Anyone that is born-again should immediately have a mind-set or set his [her] sights on the Soul-Winner's Crown or the Crown of Rejoicing.

> *"For what is our hope, or joy, or crown of rejoicing Is it not even you in the presence of our Lord Jesus Christ at His Coming?"*
>
> — 1 THESSALONIANS 2:19

Therefore, the person that wins a soul is wise. This is because what makes Heaven rejoice every day is the harvest of souls won to God. The fruit of the righteous *is a* tree of life, and he who wins souls *is* wise. Proverbs 11:30. Heaven will not fail to honour, decorate, celebrate, crown them because of these souls that are born-again into the kingdom of God.

> *"And my soul shall be joyful in the Lord; It shall rejoice in His salvation."*
>
> — PSALM 35:9

I believe every person who is saved and obey the command to witness for Jesus will be crowned with the Crown of rejoicing, which is only attained by salvation. Every believer who labours in the gospel for soul winning are candidates of the crown of rejoicing. They are the praise, and the manifestation of the glory of God those who honor the call to witness and are not ashamed of the gospel of Christ, for it is the power of God to salvation for everyone who believes. For in it the righteousness of God is revealed from faith to faith; as it is written, "The just shall live by faith."

Every committed member of the church of Jesus Christ, who witness and labor in the gospel is the glory of God, and the Crown of rejoicing will be their reward from God. "Therefore, my beloved and longed-for brethren, my joy and crown, so stand fast in the Lord, beloved." Philippians 4:1.

CROWN OF LIFE

(James 1:12, Rev. 2:10)

> *"Blessed is the man who endures temptation; for when he has been approved, he will receive the crown of life which the Lord has promised to those who love Him."*
>
> — JAMES 1:12

This Crown of Life is an honor and recognition that the Lord Jesus bestows upon those who faithfully serve and honor Him despite persecution and trials. Those who did not give up their faith but suffered and died for Christ. In some cases, it could be called the martyr's crown.

> *"Do not fear any of those things which you are about to suffer. Indeed, the devil is about to throw some of you into prison, that you may be tested, and you will have tribulation ten days. Be faithful until death, and I will give you the crown of life."*
>
> — REVELATION 2:10

Those who notwithstanding severe difficulties and great opposition were committed to finishing their race of faith. Jesus gives the crown of life to those who persevere in faith through various severe tribulation, and persecution. Those who despite great attack for their faith they encountered in this life persevere till the end.

This crown is given to those who suffered life threatening persecution for their faith. Those who suffered severe persecution for their faith. The Crown of Life for perseverance under death trial and those who died for their faith. All those Christians who are experiencing severe trials and persecution for their faith all-over the world today. Those with courage, boldness of faith persevere through, can look forward to this Crown of Life.

CROWN OF GOLD

"Reaping the Earth's Harvest Around the throne were twenty-four thrones, and seated on the thrones were twenty-four elders, clothed in white garments, with golden crowns on their heads."

— REVELATION 4:4

For You meet him with the blessings of goodness; You set a crown of pure gold upon his head. He asked life from You, and You gave it to him - Length of days forever and ever

— PSALM 21:3-4

23

IMPERISHABLE CROWN OR CROWN OF INCORRUPTION

> *"Do you not know that those who run in a race all run, but one receives the prize? Run in such a way that you may obtain it. And everyone who competes for the prize is temperate [disciplined] in all things. Now they do it to obtain a perishable crown, but we for an imperishable crown"*
>
> — 1 CORINTHIANS 9:24-25

Any individual who run a successful race in life and resisted by faith the power of the flesh are candidates to receive this awesome reward.

A HEAVENLY INHERITANCE

> *"Blessed be the God and Father of our Lord Jesus Christ, who according to His abundant mercy has begotten us again to a living hope through the resurrection of Jesus Christ from the dead to an inheritance incorruptible and undefiled and that does not fade away, reserved in heaven for you, who are kept by the power of God through faith for salvation ready to be revealed in the last time. In this you greatly rejoice, though now for a little while, if need be, you have been grieved by various trials, that the genuineness of your faith, being much more precious than gold that perishes, though it is tested by fire, may be found to praise, honour, and glory at the revelation of Jesus Christ, whom having not seen you love. Though now you do not see Him, yet believing, you rejoice with joy inexpressible and full of glory, receiving the end of your faith—the salvation of your souls."*
>
> — 1 PETER 1:3-6

Those whose flesh was tried but succeed and overcame by fire. I counsel thee to buy of me gold tried in the fire, that thou mayest be rich; ... clothed in white raiment; and they had on their heads Crowns of Gold. That will be given to those who must have kept pure and incorrupt against all opposition. The heavenly crown; for faithful endurance. The desire of every believer should be to win a heavenly reward which is "an inheritance incorruptible and undefiled and that does not fade away, reserved in heaven for you

FIVE

SIN PROBLEM

> *"Rejoicing in hope, patient in tribulation, continuing steadfastly in prayer."*
>
> — ROMANS 12:12

As Christians, we don't have religion but life and this is the life of God. We are in a relationship with God, who is our Father Lord. God does not want us to go through life with only our natural abilities. Therefore, we must be fully conscious of the truth that it is absolutely impossible to live through the Christian life with our own strength. The Jews self-righteousness failed to accept the truth demonstrating ignorance of the true righteousness of God. Trusting their own righteousness and not aware that it is not man but Christ, is the end of the law for righteousness.

"For not knowing about God's righteousness and seeking to establish their own, they did not subject themselves to the righteousness of God."

— ROMANS 10:3

Victory comes from surrender and allowing Jesus to operate and live through us. We have the mind of Christ, who is in us the hope of glory. In the scriptures our Lord exposed the self-righteous attitude in the Pharisees' prayer making himself look better to others.

The Parable of the Pharisee and the Tax Collector:

To some who were confident of their own righteousness and looked down on everyone else, Jesus told this parable: "Two men went up to the temple to pray, one a Pharisee and the other a tax collector. The Pharisee stood by himself and prayed: 'God, I thank you that I am not like other people— robbers, evildoers, adulterers - or even like this tax collector. I fast twice a week and give a tenth of all I get. But the tax collector stood at a distance. He would not even look up to heaven, but beat his breast and said, God, have mercy on me, a sinner. I tell you that this man [tax collector], rather than the other [Pharisee], went home justified before God. For all those who exalt themselves will be humbled, and those who humble themselves will be exalted."

— LUKE 18:9-14

Jesus has strong words of condemnations against the scribes and most especially the Pharisees for their hard legalistic traditions and hypocrisy.

Thank you, Lord, for opening to us the gates of righteousness; I will go through them and will praise the Lord. This is the gate of the Lord, Through which the righteous shall enter. I will praise You, For You have answered me, And have become my salvation.

Paul also dealt with this problem of self-righteousness strongly just like our Lord Jesus. In the book of Romans, he addressed the issue of the grace of God. Teaching them to stand in grace and right standing with God instead of being instructed out of the law. The self-righteous were confident that they themselves are a guide to the blind, a light to those who are in darkness, an instructor of the foolish, a teacher of babes, having the form of knowledge and truth in the law.

The Jews Guilty as the Gentiles

> "Indeed, you are called a Jew, and rest on the law, and make your boast in God, and know His will, and approve the things that are excellent, being instructed out of the law, and are confident that you yourself are a guide to the blind, a light to those who are in darkness, an instructor of the foolish, a teacher of babes, having the form of knowledge and truth in the law. You, therefore, who teach another, do you not teach yourself? You who preach that a man should not steal, do you steal? You who say, Do not commit adultery, do you commit adultery? You who abhor idols, do you rob temples? You who make your boast in the law, do you dishonour God through breaking the law? For the name of God is blasphemed among the Gentiles because of you, as it is written."
>
> — ROMANS 2:17-24

Although he taught all churches (Romans, Corinthians, Galatians) the same message using different approaches, but was very strict or tough with the Galatians condemning with strong words self-righteous and trusting in circumcision. The Galatian believers were foolish in their attempt to be perfected by the flesh. In Galatians 3:21, he says "Is the law then against the promises of God? Certainly not! For if there had been a law given which could have given life, truly righteousness would have been by the law."

The early Christians taught that they must be circumcised and perform to be acceptable to God. Apostle Paul like Jesus said those Jews made the word of God ineffective because of their tradition. He said it is another gospel "accursed" those who advocate circumcision.

> "But even if we, or an angel from heaven, preach any other gospel to you than what we have preached to you, let him be accursed. He went on saying, as we have said before, so now I say again, if anyone preaches any other gospel to you than what you have received, let him be accursed."
>
> — GALATIANS 1:8-9

Apostle Paul went more deeper and tougher saying,

> "I do not set aside the grace of God; for if righteousness comes through the law, then Christ died in vain."
>
> — GALATIANS 2:21

If righteousness could come from their own self-efforts or personal actions, then Jesus died for no actual purpose.

The voice of rejoicing and salvation is in the tents of the righteous. The right hand of the Lord does valiantly. Salvation belongs to the LORD; May Your blessing be upon Your people. Our carnal selves are deceptive, so we must stop leaning to our understanding and let the Spirit of God guide us. The children of God are led by the Holy Spirit.

> *"Trust in the Lord with all your heart And lean not on your own understanding; In all your ways acknowledge Him, And He shall direct your paths."*
>
> — PROVERBS 3:5-6

In Christ is the only way that we will ever be righteous enough to approach God. We cannot compete with the righteousness of God which is the only righteousness. It is a gift that we must attain with humility. Our act of self-righteousness is filthy in the sight of God, because we cannot earn the blessings of God. God has given us freely His righteousness in Christ Jesus.

> *"Therefore, by the deeds of the law no flesh will be justified in His sight, for by the law is the knowledge of sin."*
>
> — ROMANS 3:20

God's Righteousness is through Faith. The Lord's redemption of man was independent of works on the part of man, so God provided a solution for the necessity of righteousness. We were sinful, separated and spiritually dead, but Christ has redeemed us, granting us His Righteousness, Sonship, and Life.

> *"But now the righteousness of God apart from the law is revealed, being witnessed by the Law and the Prophets, even the righteousness of God, through faith in Jesus Christ, to all and on all who believe. For there is no difference; for all*

> *have sinned and fall short of the glory of God being justified freely by His grace through the redemption that is in Christ Jesus, whom God set forth as a propitiation by His blood, through faith, to demonstrate His righteousness, because in His forbearance God had passed over the sins that were previously committed, to demonstrate at the present time His righteousness, that He might be just and the justifier of the one who has faith in Jesus."*
>
> — ROMANS 3:20-26

God has set us free indeed, every believer should be free from the plague of self-righteousness. The behaviours of mankind is in our sin nature working hard to earn our salvation. The redeeming power of God bought for us by the precious blood of our Lord Jesus on the cross of Calvary is a perfect sacrifice. For He made Him who knew no sin to be sin for us, that we might become the righteousness of God in Him.

We take advantage and benefit from Christ sinless life and Christ sin-bearing death, that has been perfectly accomplished and does not need any more sacrifice. The truth is, it is finished, only in Christ we have God's forgiveness of sin and God's true righteousness. Self-righteousness comes from the Adamic nature, a prideful and deceitful hearts

We cannot substitute the true righteousness of God with self-effort, to do that is a sin. We should humbly accept the fact that God's grace has made available to us His Salvation and righteousness and we are commanded to look on Him, instead of on our self-abilities and self-righteousness. We look unto Jesus the author and finisher of our faith for the direction of our lives to avoid deception of the power of darkness.

Salvation is from the Lord, nobody can save himself, trusting in our own righteousness and neglecting God's gift of "righteousness in Christ Jesus" is a sin. God has freely made every believer righteous which is complete, above, beyond, and exceeding anything our own effort could guarantee.

SIX

THE RIGHTEOUS JESUS

"For He made Him who knew no sin to be sin for us, that we might become the righteousness of God in Him."

— 2 CORINTHIANS 5:21

THE ONLY SINLESS AND TOTALLY RIGHTEOUS ONE FOR YOU AND ME IS JESUS. The only one Who is wholly righteous and in Him God has made us righteous is Jesus. We are spiritually sitting with Him at the right hand of the Throne of God, and He is constantly interceding for the living saints. We are made righteous in Him and must submit to living in His righteousness. Jesus is "the firstborn from the dead", Son of the Living God, and for every born-again child of God, He became for us wisdom from God and righteousness. So that we walk in everlasting remembrance, never afraid of evil tidings, having our heart steadfast, trusting in the Lord.

Thanks be to the almighty God, we are in Christ Jesus, our perfect advocate, righteous defender, Who Has given us power to disperse abroad, to give to the poor; making our horn to be exalted with honour. And our righteousness endures forever.

Do you Know Him? Are you in Him? Is He in you?

His arms of love are stretched out to embrace you today if you will accept.

THE TEST OF KNOWING CHRIST

A letter from the heart of the Father Who is Love: "My dear children, I write this to you so that you will not sin. But if anybody does sin, we have an advocate with the Father - Jesus Christ, the Righteous One. He is the atoning sacrifice for our sins, and not only for ours but also for the sins of the whole world. We know that we have come to know him if we keep his commands. But if anybody does sin, we have an advocate with the Father - Jesus Christ, the Righteous One. He is the atoning sacrifice for our sins, and not only for ours only but also for the whole world". He alone is worthy to die for the sins of all mankind"

THE TEST OF KNOWING HIM

"Now by this we know that we know Him, if we keep His commandments"

— 1 JOHN 2:3

We are made righteous in Him and must submit to living in His righteousness.

> *"Worthy is the Lamb who was slain. To receive power and riches and wisdom, And strength and honour and glory and blessing!"*
>
> — REVELATION 5:12

Our self-righteousness is as filthy rags. There is absolutely nothing we can do on our own human effort to obtain right standing with God. Self-righteousness is only not completely totally inadequate but a sin of pride, not accepting the perfect finished work of Jesus Christ the Lord. The Scribes and most especially the Pharisees were perfect examples of self-righteousness and Jesus had strong words against this lifestyle because they believed that their righteousness was determined by their performance or outward hypocritical actions. Jesus declared that unless your righteousness exceeds that of scribes and Pharisees you will not enter the kingdom of heaven

> *"But we are all like an unclean thing, And all our righteousness's are like] filthy rags; We all fade as a leaf, And our iniquities, like the wind, Have taken us away.*
>
> — ISAIAH 64:6

Everything begins from a changed heart and not outward fake performance. We must trust in the Lord with all our heart, not leaning on our own self-righteousness. In all our actions acknowledge Jesus is Lord, and the Holy Spirit shall direct our paths. Do not be wise in your own eyes; fear the Lord and depart from evil. Our actions will reflect a changed or a new heart and renewed mind. The Word of God changes hearts. Once hearts are changed, and our minds renewed, i.e. we have "the mind of Christ" what follows is a change of action.

> *"I will give you a new heart and put a new spirit within you;*
> *I will take the heart of stone out of your flesh and give you a*
> *heart of flesh. I will put My Spirit within you and cause you*
> *to walk in My statutes, and you will keep My judgments and*
> *do them."*
>
> — EZEKIEL 36:26-27

Our actions will reveal what is in our hearts. For we all have sinned and fall short of the glory of God. There is none righteous, not one. Jesus, the righteous committed no sin, complete pure heart, without any deceit found in Him, so when we come to Him and receive His salvation, we are given His righteousness.

SEVEN

THE RIGHTEOUS MAN

> *"For the wrath of God is revealed from heaven against all ungodliness and unrighteousness of men, who suppress the truth in unrighteousness, because what may be known of God is manifest in them, for God has shown it to them."*
>
> — ROMANS 1:18-19

As it is written: "There is none righteous, no, not one;" Romans 3:10.

> *"And the gift is not like that which came through the one who sinned. For the judgment which came from one offense resulted in condemnation, but the free gift which came from many offenses resulted in justification. For if by the one man's offense death reigned through the one, much more those who*

receive abundance of grace and of the gift of righteousness will reign in life through the One, Jesus Christ.

— ROMANS 5:12-17

The revelation that through one man's offense judgment came to all men.

Therefore, as through one man's offense judgment came to all men, resulting in condemnation, even so through one Man's righteous act the free gift came to all men, resulting in justification of life. For as by one man's disobedience many were made sinners, so also by one Man's obedience many will be made righteous.

— ROMANS 5:18-21

Man needed a redeemer because he cannot redeem himself.

"Therefore, by the deeds of the law no flesh will be justified in His sight, for by the law is the knowledge of sin."

— ROMANS 3:20

Man was without hope and without God in the world.

"That at that time you were without Christ, being aliens from the commonwealth of Israel and strangers from the covenants of promise, having no hope and without God in the world."

— EPHESIANS 2:12

Man was by nature child of wrath.

> *"In which you once walked according to the course of this world, according to the prince of the power of the air, the spirit who now works in the sons of disobedience, among whom also we all once conducted ourselves in the lusts of our flesh, fulfilling the desires of the flesh and of the mind, and were by nature children of wrath, just as the others.*
>
> — EPHESIANS 2:2-3

God's love demonstrates toward us, in that while we were still sinners, Christ died for us.

> *"For scarcely for a righteous man will one die; yet perhaps for a good man someone would even dare to die. But God demonstrates His own love toward us, in that while we were still sinners, Christ died for us Much more then, having now been justified by His blood, we shall be saved from wrath through Him."*
>
> — ROMANS 5:7-9

God has delivered mankind from satan and conveyed us into the kingdom of the Son of His love.

> *"Giving thanks to the Father who has qualified us to be partakers of the inheritance of the saints in the light. He has delivered us from the power of darkness and conveyed us into the kingdom of the Son of His love, in whom we have redemption through His blood, the forgiveness of sins.*
>
> — COLOSSIANS 1:12-14

Following righteousness is life

> *"He who follows righteousness and mercy finds life, righteousness, and honour."*
>
> — PROVERBS 21:21

> *"The steps of a good man are ordered by the Lord, And He delights in his way."*
>
> — PSALM 37:23

> *"For a righteous man may fall seven times and rise again, But the wicked shall fall by calamity."*
>
> — PROVERBS 24:16

The effective, fervent prayer of a righteous man avails much

> *"Confess your trespasses to one another, and pray for one another, that you may be healed. The effective, fervent prayer of a righteous man avails much."*
>
> — JAMES 5:16

The way of the Lord is strength for the upright. The hope of the righteous will be gladness. The righteous man walks in his integrity; His children are blessed after him.

EIGHT

THE RIGHTEOUS FAMILY

Noah pleases God. He was a righteous man, blameless among the people of his time, and he walked with God.

> "This is the genealogy of Noah. Noah was a just man, perfect in his generations. Noah walked with God."
>
> — GENESIS 6:9

Right standing, Right living, is a decision of holiness, obedience, and pleasing God. This the choice of Abraham and his family, Noah and his family, Joshua, and his family, etc. Their Lifestyle is like that of those who took the decision to walk with God, in obedience and trust.

> *"For I have known him, in order that he may command his*
> *children and his household after him, that they keep the way*
> *of the Lord, to do righteousness and justice, that the Lord may*
> *bring to Abraham what He has spoken to him."*
>
> — GENESIS 18:19

These are men and women who honoured God walking in obedience and holiness. Noah found grace in the eyes of the Lord. He was righteous and lived every day in the fear of God making his way to be according to God's perfect will. Noah did; according to all that God commanded him, so he did.

Then The Lord said to Noah, come into the ark, you and all your household because I have seen that you are righteous before Me in this generation. And Noah did according to all that the Lord commanded him. The required standard of the Lord was living right every day before Him.

> *"See, I have set before you today life and good, death and*
> *evil, in that, I command you today to love the Lord your God,*
> *to walk in His ways, and to keep His commandments, His*
> *statutes, and His judgments, that you may live and multiply;*
> *and the Lord your God will bless you in the land which you*
> *go to possess. But if your heart turns away so that you do not*
> *hear, and are drawn away, and worship other gods and serve*
> *them, I announce to you today that you shall surely perish;*
> *you shall not prolong your days in the land which you cross*
> *over the Jordan to go in and possess. I call heaven and earth*
> *as witnesses today against you, that I have set before you*
> *life and death, blessing and cursing; therefore choose life,*
> *that both you and your descendants may live; that you may*
> *love the Lord your God, that you may obey His voice, and*
> *that you may cling to Him, for He is your life and the length*

of your days; and that you may dwell in the land which the Lord swore to your fathers, to Abraham, Isaac, and Jacob, to give them."

— DEUTERONOMY 30:15-20

In this lifestyle of trusting God, you and your family shall live in Divine protection. Joshua encouraged the Israelites and concluded with this statement. "But as for me and my house, we will serve the Lord" Joshua 24:15. The good news is that anyone who listens carefully to the Lord God and does what is right in His eyes, might live for righteousness.

Right living, right standing, before the almighty God saved Noah and his family from destruction in the flood. In the New Testament, the presence of Jesus Christ grace is available, righteousness is a gift not from works.

Believe on the Lord Jesus Christ, and you will be saved, you and your household. The gift of righteousness was imparted from God to everyone who is born-again through the sacrificial obedience of our Lord and Savior Jesus Christ.

"I have been crucified with Christ; it is no longer I who live, but Christ lives in me; and the life which I now live in the flesh I live by faith in the Son of God, who loved me and gave Himself for me. I do not set aside the grace of God; for if righteousness comes through the law, then Christ died in vain."

— GALATIANS 2:20-21

Our Lord Jesus offered Himself up as a sacrificial lamb of God for the sin of the whole world. However, every man must make the right choice to choose life, that is to follow Jesus.

> *"So they said, "Believe on the Lord Jesus Christ, and you will be saved, you and your household."*
>
> — ACTS 16:31

To become a disciple of Jesus Christ. You have to crucify the flesh. Have a rugged determination to yield to the leading of the Holy Sprit and dying to the desire of self or the old unrighteous self. Those who belong to Christ Jesus have crucified the flesh with its passions and desires. The flesh to be crucified is obviously the sin principle that is always present in our fallen human nature. Walk in the Spirit, and you shall not fulfil the lust of the flesh.

We crucify the flesh through complete repentance of sin, the sinful passions in our nature, and by completely renouncing the flesh. Take a step as a new creation in Christ to live by faith in obedience and love to the Son of God, who loved us and gave Himself for us. Right Standing, Right Living in Christ Jesus our Lord.

> *"The father of the righteous will rejoice, And he who begets a wise child will delight in him."*
>
> — PROVERBS 23:24

Jesus Christ is God manifest in the flesh. Without any wrongdoing on His part, took our sins in His own body on the cross of calvary. He lived in a perfect righteous relationship with God, Holy and Pure and without sin, and became our righteousness. God create a family to live on earth

> *"What is man that You are mindful of him. And the son of man that You visit him? For You have made him a little lower than the angels. And You have crowned him with glory and honour. You have made him to have dominion over the works of Your hands; You have put all things under his feet."*
>
> — PSALM 8:4-6

God's wonderful plan of salvation is by the preaching of the Gospel which changes the hearts of those who put their faith in what Jesus did for us on the cross to become righteous in Christ. There is absolutely no need for human efforts or any action to attain righteousness. Right Standing makes Right Living in Christ Jesus possible.

"Praise the Lord, Blessed are those who fear the Lord, who find great delight in his commands. Their children will be mighty in the land; the generation of the upright will be blessed. Wealth and riches are in their houses, and their righteousness endures forever. Even in darkness light dawns for the upright, for those who are gracious and compassionate and righteous. Good will come to those who are generous and lend freely, who conduct their affairs with justice. Surely the righteous will never be shaken; they will be remembered forever. They will have no fear of bad news; their hearts are steadfast, trusting in the Lord. Their hearts are secure, they will have no fear; in the end, they will look in triumph on their foes. They have freely scattered their gifts to the poor, their righteousness endures forever; their horn will be lifted high in honour."

— PSALM 112:1-9

NINE

THE RIGHTEOUS NATION

THE RIGHTEOUS NATION, IS THE NATION THAT KEEPS THE FAITH OF JESUS CHRIST. GOD almighty is the only one that can decide what is righteous. God in His infinite grace made Jesus Christ who knew no sin to be sin for us, that we might become the righteousness of God in Him. All other forms of human righteousness are as filthy as rags. Righteousness is a matter of the gift of God.

> *"Ask of Me, and I will give you the nations for your inheritance.*
> *And the ends of the earth for your possession."*
>
> — PSALM 2:8

We must continue to put our trust in God and do what we know is right, fight the good fight of faith, testify to bring the lost to repentance and to bring the Kingdom of God to bear on the affairs of nations.

> *"Blessed is the nation whose God is the LORD; The people He has chosen as His own inheritance."*
>
> — PSALM 33:12.

The righteous nation is about the people's right standing with God. This is a nation whose people have chosen to live in God's righteous standards as found in His moral law. The nation that God is the Lord is blessed. There is no mistake, the scripture is crystal clear about the outcome of our choice, because the righteousness of a nation is always exalted by the Lord, and likewise the sin of a nation is always a reproach to the Lord.

There is nothing hidden from the sight of the almighty God because His Holiness will always expose the nations to their moral and spiritual situation in their relationship with Him. The enemy of God's righteousness is sin which prevents the rays of the blessing of God.

A sinful nation is a people laden with iniquity and has forsaken the Lord. They have despised the Holy One and have turned away backwards and rejected the presence of God. The Lord will remove His hand of grace and mercy from that nation unless they repent from their sin.

> *"For He says to Moses, I will have mercy on whomever I will have mercy, and I will have compassion on whomever I will have compassion." So, then it is not of him who wills, nor of him who runs, but of God who shows mercy."*
>
> — ROMANS 9:15-16

The rebellious people who place their confidence in political leaders rather than their creator are not consecrated Christians. All ungodliness and unrighteousness of men, who would not reverence God and obey His Word, but rather suppress the truth in unrighteousness.

"For the wrath of God is revealed from heaven against all ungodliness and unrighteousness of men, who suppress the truth in unrighteousness, because what may be known of God is manifest in them, for God has shown it to them. For since the creation of the world His invisible attributes are clearly seen, being understood by the things that are made, even His eternal power and Godhead, so that they are without excuse, because, although they knew God, they did not glorify Him as God, nor were thankful, but became futile in their thoughts, and their foolish hearts were darkened."

— ROMANS 1:18-21

A nation that honors the righteous standards of God as found in His moral law is evident in the public policies and a strong conviction to live according to God's standards. Proverbs 14:12, says There is a way that seems right to a man, but its end is the way of death." God has prepared the way of salvation, so that the righteous nation which keeps the truth may enter in.

"And without controversy great is the mystery of godliness: God was manifested in the flesh, Justified in the Spirit, Seen by angels, Preached among the Gentiles, Believed on in the world, Received up in glory,"

— 1 TIMOTHY 3:16

Leaders that have the fear of God in their hearts, whose policies and actions honour the Lord are blessed. It is walking in the path as written in the scriptures that exalts a nation in righteousness. They are blessed nations because the purposed decision of their hearts is not to sin against God. Believers that are the salt of the earth are invited to keep daily, God's Word in their eyes and ears. Keeping their hearts filled with the faith of Jesus Christ. A relationship with God, living by practicing the faith lifestyle, right standing with God and true goodness.

> *"Open the gates, That the righteous nation which keeps the truth may enter in."*
>
> — ISAIAH 26:2

The people of a nation in unrighteousness have the intent of the thoughts of their heart only evil continually. They live in the culture were corruption and immorality reign. God is looking for a people of integrity, humility, honesty, and fear of the Lord. Fight the good fight by continuing to trust in God and doing what is right in His sight. Living by the truth in the Word of God, applying it in everyday life.

> *"Blessed is the nation whose God is the Lord, The people He has chosen as His own inheritance."*
>
> — PROVERBS 33:12

The moral Laws of the Lord which reflects His Nature, Holiness and Character is as relevant to us today as it was in the days of Noah, because it reveals the standard of God for righteousness to the nation. We must flee from everything that is opposed to the standard of God. Our goal should be to live in His righteousness. The scriptures encourage us to reference with childlike nature of quick to believe and to forgive, walking steadfastly in love and faith. Everyone who fears God and works righteousness is accepted by Him

"Then Peter opened his mouth and said: "In truth, I perceive that God shows no partiality. But in every nation whoever fears Him and works righteousness is accepted by Him."
— ACTS 10:34

Therefore, let us not grow weary while doing good, for in due season we shall reap if we do not lose heart. Fight the good fight of faith, lay hold on eternal life, to which you were also called and have confessed the good confession in the presence of many witnesses. Galatians 6:9, 1 Timothy 6:12. I pray that God's love and grace will reveal to the people of every nation the opportunity His Salvation, Redemption, Wisdom, and Righteousness in Christ, has provided for them to have a new beginning no matter what the mess up in their lives.

"In an acceptable time, I have heard you, And in the day of salvation, I have helped you. Behold, now is the accepted time; behold, now Is the day of salvation."
— 2 CORINTHIANS 6:2

CONFESSION SECTION

7 DAYS DECREES OF THE RIGHTEOUSNESS OF GOD

As Christians it is very essential that we believe and walk in the righteousness of God in Christ Jesus.

"He who follows righteousness and mercy Finds life, righteousness, and honour." Proverbs 21:21

"But you, O man of God, flee these things and pursue righteousness, godliness, faith, love, patience, gentleness." 1 Timothy 6:11

"Blessed are those who hunger and thirst for righteousness, for they shall be filled." Matthew 5:6

"But seek first the kingdom of God and His righteousness, and all these things shall be added to you." Matthew 6:33

"The eyes of the Lord are on the righteous, And His ears are open to their cry." Psalm 34:15

"For He made Him who knew no sin to be sin for us, that we might become the righteousness of God in Him." 2 Corinthians 5:21

"Even the righteousness of God, through faith in Jesus Christ, to all and on all who believe. For there is no difference." Romans 3:22

I pray God to give you the grace and power to be men and women of integrity, capable of doing what is right, standing and living right by the power of the Holy Spirit.

THANK YOU!

I'd like to use this time to thank you for purchasing my books and helping my ministry and work.

You have already accomplished so much, but I would appreciate an honest review of some of my books on your favourite retailer. This is critical since reviews reflect how much an author's work is respected.

Please be aware that I read and value all comments and reviews. You can always post a review even though you haven't finished the book yet and then edit your reviews later.

Thank you so much as you spare a precious moment of your time and may God bless you and meet you at the very point of your need.

Please send me an email at dr.pastormanny@gmail.com if you encounter any difficulty in leaving your review.

You can also send me an email at dr.pastormanny@gmail.com if you need prayers or counsel or if you have questions. Better still if you want to be friends with me.

OTHER BOOKS BY EMMANUEL ATOE

Church Growth in the Acts of the Apostles

The Church is the most powerful corporate body that is capable of commanding the attention of heaven on earth. The Church is God's idea and product, and so possesses an inbuilt capacity for success. The objective of this book is to get you acquainted with the purpose of the church in general, and the vision of Victory Sanctuary in particular.

A Moment of Prayer

There is nothing impossible with God but praying while breaking the law of God makes your prayers ineffective. Therefore, in this book, A Moment of Prayer, everyone under this program is expected to pray according to the rule, not against the law supporting it.

The Believer's Handbook

This book is highly recommendable for all. It is a book that will enhance your spiritual life, ignite the fire in you. It is a book that will open you heart to the mystery of faith.

The inestimable value of this book to every soul cannot be over emphasized. With this book you will get to know about the pillars of true faith in God. If you have been doubting your salvation, Christian life, the person and baptism of the Holy Ghost etc., this book is all you need.

OTHER BOOKS BY EMMANUEL ATOE

Wisdom for your Best Life

God's wisdom is an essential tool in the journey of every believer. The Bible contrasts wisdom from above, which seeks to please God and is fulfilling, from earthly wisdom, which is self-seeking and leads to ruin. The indispensability of wisdom is underscored by the biblical saying, "Wisdom is the principal thing" and "In all your getting, get wisdom."

The First Five Ps that changed my Life

The first five Ps that Changed My Life hopefully will change your life for good and for the best. Living your best life in five Ps is possible. Dr. Emmanuel O. Atoe wrote this life experiences book that is so powerful that it will change your story for good. If the principles explained in this book is applied correctly, you will achieve the desire of your heart.

Printed in the United States
by Baker & Taylor Publisher Services